LAMA CHÖPA
The Guru Puja

Composed by

Panchen Lozang Chökyi Gyaltsen

the first Panchen Lama

Translated into English by
Robert Preece

Introductory remarks by
Geshe Thubten Jinpa & Zasep Tulku Rinpoche

LAMA CHÖPA
The Guru Puja
Panchen Lozang Chökyi Gyaltsen
Translated by Robert Preece

Translation © Robert Preece 2012
All rights reserved

Design by Karma Yönten Gyatso
Music transcription by Justin Wah Kan
Mudra photos by Jeffrey Wah Kan

Cover photo © v33sean, Shutterstock

Published by
The Sumeru Press Inc.
PO Box 2089, Richmond Hill, ON
Canada L4E 1A3

ISBN 978-1-896559-11-7 (pocket edition)

For more information about The Sumeru Press
visit us at *www.sumeru-books.com*

Twenty-five percent of profits from sales of this book go towards development projects at Tashi Lhunpo Monastery, India, the Panchen Lama's seat in exile.

For more information about their work, visit them at *www.tashilhunpo.org*

Contents

5	Preface
7	Foreword
9	Translator's Introduction
11	Performance Notes
16	Refuge
18	The Tree of Assembled Gurus
22	The Prayer of Seven Limbs
29	Requests
33	Tsog Offering
40	A Song to Move the Dakinis' Hearts
45	Offering Tsog to the Local Spirits
47	Dedication & Verses for Auspiciousness
50	About the Translator

Preface

It is a real delight to read the famed *Lama Chöpa* in Rob Preece's new translation. In chanting the lines from this new rendering, one could almost hear echoes of the original Tibetan composed so eloquently by Panchen Lobsang Chögyen, one of Tibet's greatest spiritual masters.

Thupten Jinpa, PhD.,
principal English translator
to H.H. the Dalai Lama and
the author/translator of
Essential Mind Training
Montreal, QC
2012

Foreword

Lama Chöpa is a practice of guru devotion special to the Gelugpa tradition of Tibetan Buddhism. In Sanskrit, *lama* is *guru*, and *chöpa* is *offering*, so *Lama Chöpa* translates into English as "offering to the spiritual guide." In the Gelugpa tradition, there are many guru yoga sadhanas, but *Lama Chöpa* is the most popular and sacred text. A special practice of Je Tsongkhapa (1357-1419), the founder of the Gelugpa School, *Lama Chöpa* was compiled by the first Panchen Lama, Panchen Lozang Chökyi Gyaltsen (1570-1662), who was the teacher of the fifth Dalai Lama (1617-1682). *Lama Chöpa* became so popular in Tibet and Mongolia that almost every monk of the Gelugpa tradition had it memorized, and recited it on a daily basis, both in the temple as a group practice, and individually.

Lama Chöpa is considered to be an Anuttarayoga Tantra or Highest Yoga Tantra practice. As indicated by the opening words, "Arising within the sphere of great bliss, I manifest as a Guru Yidam," it contains the idea of personal transformation through the practitioner merging his or her mind with the guru as the meditational deity. The essence of the practice is to see the guru as an Enlightened Being, a Buddha, and to receive his or her blessings in return.

The practice begins with Refuge prayers and the visualization of the Refuge Tree. The practice continues with the Prayer of the Seven Limbs, recitation of all the stages of Lamrim, or the Gradual Path to

Enlightenment, followed by a Tsog Offering, and Dedication and Auspicious Prayers. One of the unique things about *Lama Chöpa* as opposed to the other guru yoga sadhanas is that it can be combined with each of the Anuttarayoga Yoga practices of Heruka, Yamantaka, and Guhyasamaja. Je Pabongkha Rinpoche wrote three separate texts combining *Lama Chöpa* with sadhanas of each of these yidams.

Lama Chöpa is a profoundly beautiful and poetic practice. Not only is the text exquisitely phrased, but when chanted according to the beautiful traditional melodies, it gives an uplifting feeling and generates deep devotion to guru and yidam. All negative minds are transcended.

I believe that the daily practice of *Lama Chöpa* alone is sufficient to increase dharma realizations and overcome all kinds of obstacles; meditation on *Lama Chöpa* leads to the state of enlightenment. No other practice is needed.

Zasep Tulku Rinpoche
Nelson, BC
2012

Translator's Introduction

This version of Lama Chöpa came into being while I was in retreat high above McLeod Gange in Northern India between 1980 and 1985. Having a desire to do this practice, but feeling frustrated by the English versions that were available, I wanted to find a way to actually chant the practice rather than simply read it. As a result I spent many enjoyable hours in breaks between meditation sessions looking out over the foothills towards Dharamsala singing to myself and gradually transposing the text to music.

As far as possible most of the tunes accord with the original Tibetan chants with one or two variations that I felt brought the text alive in a slightly different way. I am aware that my translation is not perfect in its rendering of the original Tibetan and in places I have tried to be true to the meaning while needing to create a more chantable meter. When it was completed Lama Yeshe would often ask for it to be performed at Tushita retreat centre in Dharamsala when Westerners performed Tsog.

My hope is that being able to chant Lama Chöpa in English in this way can bring a real heart connection to the practice.

Rob Preece
Devon, England
2012

Performance Notes

In order to benefit fully from the liturgical elements of this edition of The Lama Chöpa, it is important to understand some of the typographic, musical and performance components within the text.

Sections
Major sections are indicated by larger bold type. Subsections are indicated by bold type the same size as the text, but placed in square brackets.

In order not to break passages, we have tried to end sections at ends of pages to avoid awkward transitions from one section to another.

Music
The melody for each section precedes the text for that section. The melody is correct, but the number of beats may vary from line to line based on the number of syllables to be sung. Once you understand the basic flow of the music, you'll be able to adjust accordingly.

Additionally, there is a fair bit of latitude in the singing of grace notes, ornamental variations, etc.

In some cases, a variant melody may be sung for the first line of a section. In those cases, a more extensive set of melody lines is included in the section.

If you find the key difficult to sing, feel free to change it, and just keep the relationships between the notes the same.

Mantras
These are presented in capital letters and are meant to be spoken, or chanted in a monotone that drops and extends on the last syllable.

There are three exceptions to this. In the Refuge section, the Refuge mantra to the Guru, Buddha, Dharma and Sangha is chanted according to the melody included above it. In the Tsog Offering, the mantra melodies are provided. In the Song to Move the Dakinis' Hearts, the AH LA LA mantra beginning each stanza is sung in the same melody as the text that follows it.

Mudras
Photos of the appropriate ritual hand gestures have been inserted into the text at the relevant points.

Spoken word
Some passages are meant to be spoken rather than sung. These parts are presented in italics.

Performance instructions
Indented italic text in parentheses contains performance instructions that are not meant to be spoken. They are there to tell you when to repeat a section, when to speed up or slow down the pace of the chanting, or when to perform a particular mudra action.

Performance dates
Lama Chöpa is often performed in an abridged version on a daily or weekly basis. However, the Tsog Offering is usually only performed in the evening, twice a month, on

the quarter moon (half-way between the new moon and the full moon and then half-way between the full moon and the new moon).

A final word
The Lama Chöpa is meant to be a profoundly meaningful and emotionally enriching experience. The goal is for you to deeply experience the joy of the text. Feel free to be creative with the ritual in any way that assists you in your personal journey to understanding.

Karma Yönten Gyatso
Publisher

LAMA CHÖPA
The Guru Puja

Panchen Lozang Chökyi Gyaltsen

Refuge

Arising within the sphere of great bliss
I manifest as a Guru Yidam.
From my clear body light in profusion
radiates forth throughout the ten directions,
blessing all places and beings therein.
All becomes most perfectly arrayed with
only qualities infinitely pure.

From an exalted, wise and virtuous mind,
I and all mother beings vast as space,
from now until our full Enlightenment,
seek refuge in the Gurus and Three Jewels.

(Slower. Repeat 3 x.)

NAMO GURUBHYAH
NAMO BUDDHAYA
NAMO DHARMAYA
NAMO SANGHAYA

(Normal speed. Repeat 3 x.)

For the sake of all mother sentient beings
I transform into a Guru Yidam,
and thus shall I lead all sentient beings
to a Guru Yidam's Enlightenment.

For the sake of all mother sentient beings
I shall swiftly in this very lifetime
become a primordial Guru Yidam.
To lead mother sentient beings from suffering
into the supreme bliss of Buddhahood,
I now shall practice the most profound path,
the essence of Guru Yidam yoga.

OM AH HUM
OM AH HUM
OM AH HUM

Pure clouds of outer, inner and secret offerings, objects which bind us close and fields of vision, pervade the reaches of space and earth and sky, spreading out beyond the range of thought. In essence they are pristine awareness, in aspect inner offerings and various objects of offering. Their function is to generate the extraordinary pristine awareness of voidness and bliss as objects to be enjoyed by the six senses.

Panchen Lozang Chökyi Gyaltsen

The Tree of Assembled Gurus

Dwelling in the vast heavens
of bliss and voidness unified
amidst billowing clouds of
Samantabhadra offerings,
cresting a wish-granting tree
embellished with leaves, flowers and fruit,
rests a lion throne ablaze
with ornate forms of precious gems.

Upon lotus, sun and full moon
sits my Guru, kind in all three ways;
in essence you're all Buddhas,
in aspect a saffron-robed monk;
having one face and two arms,
you bear a white and radiant smile.
Your right hand is in the gesture
of expounding the Dharma;
your left in equipoise mudra
cradles a bowl of nectar;
draped with three robes of saffron,
crowned by a golden pandit's hat.

Within your heart is the
all-pervading Lord Vajradhara,
with a body blue in colour,
having one face and two arms,
with vajra and bell embracing

Lama Chöpa

Vajradhatu Ishvari.
They delight in the play of
simultaneous bliss and void,
adorned with jeweled ornaments
and garments of heavenly silk.

Emblazoned with the major and
minor marks of a Buddha,
radiant with thousands of light rays,
you sit in the vajra pose;
brilliantly you are enhaloed
by a five-colored rainbow.
Totally pure, your skandhas are
the five Buddhas Gone to Bliss;
Your four elements are the
four motherly wisdom consorts.

Your five sense bases,
your energy channels, sinews and joints
are all in reality the eight noble Bodhisattvas.
All the hairs of your pores
are the twenty-one thousand Arhats.
Your limbs are the powerful
and mighty wrathful Protectors.
The light rays direction guardians,
lords of wealth and attendants;
while all the worldly gods
are but cushions for your lotus feet.

Surrounding you in their order
is an encircling sea

of actual and lineage Gurus,
Yidams and mandala deities,
Buddhas, Bodhisattvas, Viras,
Dakinis and Protectors.

The three doors of each are marked
with the three adorning vajras.
From their syllables HUM
light rays go out and hook-like draw forth
wisdom beings from their abode,
that they may become united.

O, you who are the everlasting source
of all goodness, bliss and perfection,
O, root and lineage Gurus, Yidams,
Three Sublime Jewels, Viras, Dakinis,
Dharmapalas and all Protectors,
with entourage and of the three times,
by the power of your compassion
please come forth and steadfastly remain.

Though all things are totally free of
any inherent coming and going,
still you arise through virtuous conduct
of wisdom and loving compassion,
in whatsoever form is suiting
the temperament of your disciples.
O, most Holy Refuge Protectors
please come forth with your vast entourage.

Lama Chöpa

OM GURU BUDDHA
BODHISATTVA
DHARMAPALA
SAPARIWARA
EH HYE HIH

DZA

HUM

BAM

HO

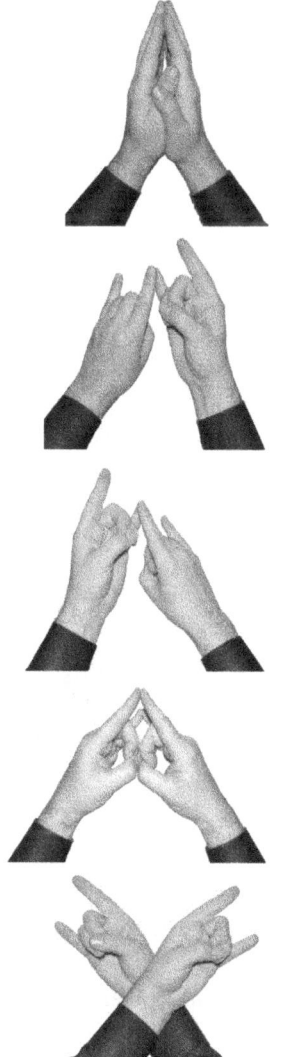

The wisdom and symbolic beings become nondual.

   (Snap your fingers once.)

Panchen Lozang Chökyi Gyaltsen

The Prayer of Seven Limbs

[1. Prostration]

Your jewel-like bodies through compassion
bestow in an instant even the
supreme attainment of three kayas,
the sphere of simultaneous great bliss.
O, supreme Vajradhara Gurus
at your lotus feet I humbly bow.

Pristine awareness of all Buddhas,
you play the role of a saffron-robed monk,
as a supreme skilful means to appear
in whichever way suits your disciples.
O, sublime Holy Refuge Protectors
at your lotus feet I humbly bow.
The only source of benefit and bliss,
you clearly eliminate the root
of all delusions and their instincts.
Treasury of jewel-like qualities,
O, the most Venerable Gurus
at your lotus feet I humbly bow.

You are the essence of all Buddhas,
teachers of all including the gods,
source of eighty-four thousand Dharmas,
towering over a host of Aryas.

Lama Chöpa

O, supremely benevolent Gurus
at your lotus feet I humbly bow.

To all you Venerable Gurus
of the three times and ten directions,
to the Three Rare and Supreme Jewels
and to all who are worthy of homage,
with faith, esteem and seas of lyric praise,
manifest countlessly I humbly bow.

[2. Offerings]

Refuge Protectors with your entourage
oceans of clouds of offerings we present.

From vast well-fashioned precious vessels
flow forth gently four streams of pure nectar.

Flowers and trees, bouquets and garlands
exquisitely fill the earth and the sky.

The heavens billow with blue summer clouds —
lazulite smoke from sweet, fragrant incense.

The light from suns, moons, jewels and flaming lamps
dispels darkness of countless billion worlds.

Vast seas of perfume swirl out endlessly —
fragrant camphor, saffron and sandalwood.

Panchen Lozang Chökyi Gyaltsen

Delightful food of a hundred flavors,
feasts of gods and men, mass a Mount Meru.

Music coming from diverse instruments
blends in harmonies filling the three realms.

Outer and inner five-sense goddesses
with their offerings pervade all directions.

[Short Mandala Offering]

O, the ground with scent
is blessed
and with flowers strewn,
adorned with Mount Meru,
the four lands,
the sun and moon,
transformed as a Pure Land
and then offered.
May all wandering beings
enjoy this Buddha Realm.

Lama Chöpa

All those objects
of my mind's three poisons,
coveted friend, foe and stranger,
body, wealth, worldly pleasures,
without a feeling of loss, we surrender.
Receive them please
and free all beings from their bondage.

IDAM GURU RATNA MANDALAKAM NIRYATAYAMI

(Release mandala offering mandala.)

Refuge Protectors, wealth of compassion,
eminent and supreme merit field,
we present you with pure devotion
countless Mount Merus and continents,
the seven precious royal emblems,
the precious minor symbols and more,
delightful realms and those that dwell therein,
treasuries of wealth of gods and men.

Panchen Lozang Chökyi Gyaltsen

To please you Venerable Gurus
we offer you these diverse objects,
both actual and those envisioned;
a pleasure grove all-captivating,
on the shores of a wish-granting sea
strewn with thousand-petalled lotuses.

These are the offerings arising
from white virtues worldly and divine.
Flowers in profusion scattered everywhere
are the virtues of the three gateways
of ourselves and those of all others
dwelling in this world and those beyond.
It is infused with myriad fragrances
of Samantabhadra offerings,
laden with fruit of the three trainings,
the Two Stages and the Five Great Paths.

We offer lightly-scented China tea,
a libation the colour of saffron,
steeped in a hundred subtle flavors.
This, as five hooks, five lamps and so forth,
is purified, transformed and increased
into a vast ocean of nectar.

We offer consorts fair and beautiful,
a host of messenger Dakinis,
born of place, mantra and simultaneously,
having graceful and slender figures,
aglow with radiant, youthful vibrance,
skilled in the sixty-four arts of love.

Lama Chöpa

We offer the void sphere of all things,
supreme, ultimate Bodhicitta,
beyond all words, thought and expression —
spontaneous, indivisible,
free of notions of true existence —
pristine clearness unified with bliss.

We offer various potent medicines,
cure for the four hundred afflictions.
Your pleasing servants, we devote ourselves.
Pray keep us as long as heavens endure.

[3. Confession]

We now lay bare with regretful mind,
before the eyes of those Greatly Compassionate Ones,
whatsoever deeds unwholesome,
bound to misfortune, committed from beginningless time,
those rejoiced in or caused in others,
and so we vow never to commit them again.

[4. Rejoicing]

Though all things like dream illusions
have no inherent or natural existence,
we sincerely rejoice in the joys
and happiness of all Aryas and worldly beings,
and in every white and virtuous deed
that has ever arisen throughout the three times.

[5. Requesting the Turning of the Dharma Wheel]

May the rains of Dharma vast and profound
descend from a hundred thousand clouds billowing —
sublime wisdom, loving kindness,
to thereby nurture, sustain and propagate
a garden of radiant moon flowers
for the benefit and bliss of limitless beings.

[6. Requesting the Guru to Remain]

Your immortal vajra body
is a vessel of union's mighty victory.
To accord with all our wishes,
we request you to abide with us forever,
by sustaining emanations,
pass not beyond sorrow until samsara's end.

[7. Dedication of Merit]

The collection of white virtues
thereby created we sincerely dedicate,
that we may be, throughout all our lives,
inseparably protected by noble Gurus,
who possess the three great kindnesses,
thus may we attain Vajradhara's unity.

Requests

We make our requests to you,
Holders of Elders' Vinaya,
Masters, second Buddhas clad
in saffron, source of excellence,
Treasury of jewels of learning,
ocean of moral discipline.

We make our requests to you,
Lords of Mahayana Dharma,
Envoys of the Conquerors,
having the ten rare qualities,
rendering you perfect guides
on the path of Those Gone to Bliss.

Panchen Lozang Chökyi Gyaltsen

We make our requests to you,
foremost Holders of the Vajra,
bearing twenty skills of Tantra,
masters of speech and composing,
honourable, without pretension,
patient with your three doors subdued.

We make our requests to you,
O compassionate Protectors.
With precision you impart
the good way of Those Gone to Bliss
to those of degenerate times,
untamed by Buddhas of the past.

We make our requests to you,
O compassionate Protectors.
You enact the Victors' deeds
for those who lack a Protector
at this time when the sun-like teachings
of the Sage are setting.

We make our requests to you,
O compassionate Protectors.
Just one single hair from your pores
is for us a merit-field,
more praiseworthy than
the Victors of three times and ten regions.

Lama Chöpa

We make our requests to you,
O compassionate Protectors,
manifest in earthly guise,
a weave of illusion-like skilful means
having three adorning wheels
of Those Thus Gone you lead beings.

We make our requests to you,
essence of the Three Supreme Jewels.
In nature your aggregates, senses,
limbs and elements are
Lords and Consorts, Bodhisattvas,
Guardians of Five Families.

We make our requests to you,
foremost Holders of the Vajra,
Lords omniscient of all Families,
hosts of primordial unity,
play of pristine awareness,
essence of countless mandalas.

We make our requests to you,
Immaculate Samantabhadra,
the Ultimate Bodhicitta,
free of beginning or end,
the pervading nature of
all things in motion and at rest,
inseparable from the undefiled play
of simultaneous bliss.

Panchen Lozang Chökyi Gyaltsen

[Single-Pointedly Requesting]

You are our Gurus; you are our Yidams;
you are our Dakinis and Dharmapalas.
From this moment until our Enlightenment,
we shall seek no refuge other than you.
In this life, the bardo and all future lives,
hold us all with your hook of compassion.
Free us from samsara and Nirvana's fears,
grant us all your supreme attainment.
Be our steadfast friend and guard us
against all harmful interferences.

   (Repeat 3 x.)

By the force of having thus requested three times, nectars and rays — white, red and dark blue — stream forth from the centers of our Guru's body, speech and mind, one by one and then all together. They absorb into our own three centers one by one and finally together. Thereby the four obstacles are purged and the four empowerments are implanted, and the seeds of the four kayas received. Then a smiling emanation of the Guru, coming forth, dissolves into us and we are blessed with his inspiration.

   (Recite mantras of your Guru, your Deity, Vajradhara, and seed syllables.)

Lama Chöpa

Tsog Offering

OM AH HUM   OM AH HUM   OM AH HUM

Pure clouds of outer, inner and secret offerings, objects which bind us close and fields of vision, pervade the reaches of space and earth and sky spreading out beyond the range of thought. In essence they are pristine awareness, in aspect inner offerings and various objects of offering. Their function is to generate the extraordinary pristine awareness of voidness and bliss as objects to be enjoyed by the six senses.

EH MA HO...
Within the grand play of the pristine awareness,
all places are vajra fields; structures, vajra palaces.
Oceans of clouds billow forth Samantabhadra offerings.

All objects are imbued with the glories of all wishes;
all beings are actual great Viras and Virinis.
Without even words impure, all is infinitely pure.

HUM...
From a state of Dharmakaya stilled of mental conception,
upon a turbulent wind and a powerful blazing fire,
resting on the crown of a tripod of three human heads,
AH... in a human skullcup,
OM... the ingredients appear.

Above them are OM AH HUM
sparkling with brilliant colour.
The wind blows, the fire flares
and the ingredients melt.
From these boiling substances
copious vapors tumble forth.

Then from the three syllables
light in profusion radiates
out in the ten directions
drawing forth the three Vajras
with nectar which then dissolves
into the three syllables.
These melt into nectar and
blend with the ingredients,
purifying, transforming
and increasing EH MA HO.
Thus an ocean of splendor
of all that could be wished for.

OM AH HUM
OM AH HUM
OM AH HUM

Lama Chöpa

O, hosts of Root and Lineage Gurus,
Yidams, Assemblies of Deities,
the Three Supreme Jewels of Refuge,
Viras, Dakinis, Dharmapalas:
I request you, by your compassion,
come forth to this place of offering.

Place your radiant feet firmly upon
this elegant throne formed of jewels,
amidst a vast ocean of clouds of
outer, inner and secret offerings.
Grant us striving for realizations,
powerful attainments we wish for.

Panchen Lozang Chökyi Gyaltsen

HO...
This ocean of offering tsog of undefiled nectar,
blessed by samadhi, mantra and mudra,
we offer in order to please you
hosts of root and lineage Gurus.

OM AH HUM...
Contented by your sport with
all these splendors that could be wished for,

EH MA HO...
Please let fall a great rain of blessings.

HO...
This ocean of offering tsog of undefiled nectar,
blessed by samadhi, mantra and mudra,
we offer in order to please you
hosts of Yidams with your entourage.

OM AH HUM...
Contented by your sport with
all these splendors that could be wished for,

EH MA HO...
Please let fall a rain of powerful attainments.

HO...
This ocean of offering tsog of undefiled nectar,
blessed by samadhi, mantra and mudra,
we offer in order to please you
hosts of Precious Jewels of Refuge.

OM AH HUM...
Contented by your sport with
all these splendors that could be wished for,

EH MA HO...
Please let fall a great rain of sacred Dharma.

HO...
This ocean of offering tsog of undefiled nectar,
blessed by samadhi, mantra and mudra,
we offer in order to please you
hosts of Dakinis and Dharmapalas.

OM AH HUM...
Contented by your sport with
all these splendors that could be wished for,

EH MA HO...
Please let fall a great rain of virtuous conduct.

HO...
This ocean of offering tsog of undefiled nectar,
blessed by samadhi, mantra and mudra,
we offer in order to please you
hosts of beings who were once our mothers.

OM AH HUM...
Contented by your sport with
all these splendors that could be wished for,

EH MA HO...
Please still the sufferings from distorted views.

Lama Chöpa

[Offering to the Guru]

(Very slowly.)
EH MA HO...
Here is a great circle of tsog.
You who have followed in the footsteps of
all the Buddhas of the three times.
Realizing that you are the source of all
powerful attainments, O great Vira-hero,
you who have freed yourself
from all superstitions,
we invite you continually to enjoy
this circle of tsog.
AH LA LA HO

OM...
I visualize myself as a Guru Yidam
with a nature inseparable from the three Vajras.

AH...
This nectar of uncontaminated, pristine awareness

HUM...
Without moving from a state of Bodhicitta,
I play with, to satisfy the deities within my form.

AH HO MAHASUKHA
(Release the prayer mudra. Taste the tsog.)

Panchen Lozang Chökyi Gyaltsen

A Song to Move the Dakinis' Hearts

HUM...
We make our requests to you,
Tathagatas gone beyond,
Great Viras and Yoginis,
all Dakas and Dakinis.

Heruka delights in supreme bliss,
thereby becomes intoxicated;
by this blissful intoxication
brings satisfaction to the Consort;
to accord with precepts of practice
entering the union of innate bliss.

AH LA LA, LA LA HO, AH E A AH, A RA LI HO
You the vast multitudes of
immaculate Dakinis,
look upon us all with love;
bestow powerful attainments.

HUM...
We make our requests to you,
Tathagatas gone beyond,
Great Viras and Yoginis,
all Dakas and Dakinis.

Through inspiring the mind of great bliss
and the moving dance of their bodies,
there arises the play of great bliss
within the lotus of the Consort.
This bliss we offer to you
multitudes of powerful Yoginis.

AH LA LA, LA LA HO, AH E A AH, A RA LI HO
You the vast multitudes of
immaculate Dakinis,
look upon us all with love;
bestow powerful attainments.

HUM...
We make our requests to you,
Tathagatas gone beyond,
Great Viras and Yoginis,
all Dakas and Dakinis.

Yoginis who dance so sensually,
with enchanting and graceful movements,
the Protector so fully to please,
and the multitudes of Dakinis,
come before us and inspire us all.
Bestow upon us innate great bliss.

AH LA LA, LA LA HO, AH E A AH, A RA LI HO
You the vast multitudes of
immaculate Dakinis,
look upon us all with love;
bestow powerful attainments.

HUM...
We make our requests to you,
Tathagatas gone beyond,
Great Viras and Yoginis,
all Dakas and Dakinis.

Great bliss which is endowed with
countless liberating qualities,
without which freedom cannot be gained
though one endures great austerity —
that sublime bliss so abides within
the centre of the supreme lotus.

AH LA LA, LA LA HO, AH E A AH, A RA LI HO
You the vast multitudes of
immaculate Dakinis,
look upon us all with love;
bestow powerful attainments.

HUM...
We make our requests to you,
Tathagatas gone beyond,
Great Viras and Yoginis,
all Dakas and Dakinis.

Just as a lotus born out of mud,
great bliss though evolving from desire
is unsullied by its defilements
arising immaculately pure.
May samsara's bonds be swiftly loosed
by your lotus bliss great Yoginis.

AH LA LA, LA LA HO, AH E A AH, A RA LI HO
You the vast multitudes of
immaculate Dakinis,
look upon us all with love;
bestow powerful attainments.

HUM...
We make our requests to you,
Tathagatas gone beyond,
Great Viras and Yoginis,
all Dakas and Dakinis.

Just as swarming bees will so draw forth
the purest nectar of fragrant flowers
may we too be fully satisfied
by the captivating nectar of
the lotus in full maturity,
possessing six refined qualities.

AH LA LA, LA LA HO, AH E A AH, A RA LI HO
You the vast multitudes of
immaculate Dakinis,
look upon us all with love;
bestow powerful attainments.

HUM...
*Impure deceptive appearances
become purified in the sphere of voidness.*

AH...
*This magnificent nectar
created out of pristine awareness*

OM...
*Becomes a vast ocean
of all desired things.*

OM AH HUM
OM AH HUM
OM AH HUM

Offering Tsog to the Local Spirits

HO...
This ocean of remaining tsog of undefiled nectar,
blessed by samadhi, mantra and mudra,
we offer in order to please you
hosts of oath-bound ground protectors.

OM AH HUM...
Contented by your sport with
all these splendors that could be wished for,

EH MA HO...
Please fulfill your pledged virtuous yogic conduct.

(Take the pretas' tsog outside.)

HO...
By offering this ocean of remaining tsog to the guests who are left, together with their entourage, may the precious teachings proliferate. May the upholders of the teachings, the offering patrons, together with their entourage, and especially we yogis — may we all gain freedom from sickness, a long life, fame, good fortune and abundant wealth.

Bestow on us the powerful attainments of actions such as pacification, increase and so forth. O, oath-bound Protectors, protect us! Help us obtain all powerful attainments.

Make us meet no untimely death, sickness, demons or interfering spirits. See that we have no bad dreams, ill omens or calamities.

May we have worldly happiness, good crops and harvests. May the Dharma flourish, all goodness and joy come about, and may all wishes within our minds be fulfilled.

And by the force of this bountiful giving, may I become a self-made Buddha for the sake of all beings, and by my generosity may I liberate the multitudes of beings who were not liberated by the Buddhas of old.

Dedication

White virtues we have thus created
we dedicate as the causes for
us to uphold the Holy Dharma
of Scriptures and most profound Insights,
fulfilling every prayer and action
of the three times' Buddhas and their kin.

May we by the force of this virtue
never be parted in all our lives
from the four spheres of Mahayana,
reaching our journey's end by way of
Renunciation, Bodhicitta,
the Perfect View and the Two Stages.

Verses for Auspiciousness

Through the power of whatever
white virtues within samsara and Nirvana,
from all hardship and misfortune,
may all be auspicious for us to be now free
to enjoy a perfect treasure
of all good fortune both temporal and ultimate.

O omniscient Lozang Dragpa,
may all be auspicious for teachings to endure,
through your centers of pure practice,
being filled with assembled yogis, monks and nuns,
who are striving single-pointedly
to completely accomplish the three pure trainings.

Thus requested, Lozang Dragpa,
who from your youth made requests
to the Guru Yidam,
for you now to grant our wishes,
may all be auspicious, O Lozang Vajradhara.

Like a lake that swells in times of rain,
may all be auspicious for our richness to grow,
thereby bringing an unbroken flow
of births of leisure within faultless families,
our days filled with Holy Dharma,
thus delighting in the glories of perfection.

By whatever virtues we have done
and shall do from now until our Enlightenment,
may your body of form thus remain
within this land like a vajra immutable.
We entreat you, by your kindness,
may all be auspicious, Holy Venerable One.

TASHI SHO

*(Throw a few grains of rice
as a blessing.)*

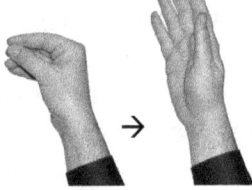

About the Translator

ROB PREECE
(BSc. Adv. Dip. Transpersonal Psychology UKCP reg.)

Following a four-year apprenticeship in electronics engineering, Rob went to university to study psychology. It was at this time he met both the work of C.G. Jung and Buddhism. In 1973, after a period of travel, he met Lama Thubten Yeshe and Lama Zopa Rinpoche in Nepal. Since that time he has been a practicing Tibetan Buddhist.

After working as a social worker, Rob was part of a small group that founded a Buddhist centre in the UK for his Tibetan teachers. For the next four years he studied the foundations of Tibetan practice in that Buddhist community. In 1980 he returned to India and was in retreat for much of the next five years. This gave him a chance to explore the practices of the Tantric tradition in some depth, meditating under the guidance of Lama Yeshe, Zopa Rinpoche and Gen Jhampa Wangdu in particular. While in India, he was fortunate enough to receive teachings on many of the important aspects of Tibetan Buddhism, in particular Tantric teachings, from Lamas such as H.H. Dalai Lama, Song Rinpoche and many others. It also gave him the opportunity to learn Thangkha (Tantric Icon) painting.

Returning to the west, he at first lived as a Thangkha painter and then in 1985 he trained as a psychotherapist principally with the Center for Transpersonal

Psychology. This began the process of bringing together the two worlds of Buddhist and Western psychology. He has been a practicing psychotherapist since 1988, gradually developing a style that is a synthesis of Buddhist and Jungian understanding.

Since 1985 he has been leading meditation retreats following the instruction and guidance of his teachers. Lama Yeshe was particularly influential is this, supporting his integration of a more Western approach. This has meant gradually guiding people through a kind of apprenticeship in the practice of Tantra. Increasingly Rob has become involved in what he now calls spiritual mentoring, bringing together his experience of both Eastern and Western approaches. This has also led to writing *The Psychology of Buddhist Tantra* and *The Wisdom of Imperfection*.

He leads many meditation retreats in the UK, some of which incorporate a movement practice facilitated by his wife Anna. As a father of two sons, an experienced Thangkha painter and a keen gardener, he tries to ground Buddhist practice in a creative practical lifestyle.

For further information about Rob's work, go to his website at *www.mudra.co.uk*